Thaise Lorena Santos da Silva
Antonio E. F. Romero

Homosexual Adoption

Thaise Lorena Santos da Silva
Antonio E. F. Romero

Homosexual Adoption

A Legal and Sociological Approach

ScienciaScripts

Cover image: www.ingimage.com

This book is a translation from the original published under ISBN 978-3-330-73685-6.

Publisher:
Sciencia Scripts
is a trademark of
Dodo Books Indian Ocean Ltd. and OmniScriptum S.R.L publishing group

120 High Road, East Finchley, London, N2 9ED, United Kingdom
Str. Armeneasca 28/1, office 1, Chisinau MD-2012, Republic of Moldova, Europe
Printed at: see last page
ISBN: 978-620-8-03124-4

INDEX

1. A BRIEF HISTORY OF SOCIAL MOVEMENTS IN BRAZIL

Social movements have accompanied the democratic steps of various nations, including Brazil, over the last few decades, constantly present in important historical events, especially in the area of social conquests. In fact, they are a mechanism that citizens use to claim and have their collective interests and desires recognized.

The influence of social movements goes far beyond the political effects they produce, as their support determines changes in behavior and rules on the part of individuals. What's more, there is a much more complex symbolic dimension on which social movements have a major impact: social transformation. Today, on the basis of these new mobilizations, citizens and societies are combining the grammar of gender equality, ecological concerns, environmental conservation and the rights of the unborn, which were unthinkable before the emergence of social movements with these new agendas.

For Correia (2001), civil society uses social movements to win rights that are denied or not made available by the state. It is in this context of deprivation, exclusion and social needs that the daily practices of social movements are situated. Although they act with certain limitations, they are potential means of new ways of doing politics, of social participation, of building the democratic process and of social transformation. It is assumed that social movements are collective and organized attempts aimed at seeking certain changes or even stipulating the possibility of building a new social order.

Around the 1960s and 1970s, popular and social movements spread in Brazil. From the end of the 1970s, the trade union movement and student organizations gained strength. Strikes by metalworkers paralyzed the industries of Sao Paulo, soon followed by strikes by bank workers. The crisis of the *"economic miracle"* was the trigger for these movements, and the fight against famine shook the foundations of the dictatorship. At the same time, groups linked to specific issues emerged: women, indigenous peoples, blacks and homosexuals.

When studying the history of social movements and their main theoretical frameworks, it becomes clear that most of them, up until the 1960s, focused on issues relating to the struggles of the workers' movement (the trade union movement).

With the advent of struggles for social rights (gender, sex, race, culture, ethnicity, etc.) in the 1950s and 1960s in Europe and the United States, studies on social movements were based on new paradigms. Elements related to the subjective dimensions and value systems of these groups began to be analyzed.

In Brazil, the struggle for the right to citizenship (the exercise of rights and duties) by excluded sectors of society has expanded into struggles for the right to freedom, equality and the expression of individuality. Driven by the re-democratization movement, groups representing these new social movements organized themselves to demonstrate their desire to build a society without exclusions, discrimination and segmentation. Among these, we highlight the fight for gay rights.

It is essential to consider the great importance of social movements in the Brazilian democratic process, through their actions aimed at claiming rights which, until now, have not been available to citizens. In this way, the struggles unleashed in civil society are absolutely essential in a process of effective social transformation, on the road to human emancipation.

2. HOMOSEXUAL MOVEMENT IN BRAZIL

The 1960s marked a peculiar period in the history of the twentieth century, with a series of demonstrations and challenges to established values. This period saw the emergence, among others, of the *hippie* and feminist movements, and homosexuals also began to organize themselves in a more articulate way, initially in the United States and Europe. This was a time when established values and morals were questioned through demonstrations and attitudes that denoted a feeling of sexual liberation.

In 1966, American homosexuals demonstrated against the expulsion of gays from the armed forces. The idea of sexual liberation was incorporated into the counter-culture movement, along with black and feminist activists, giving rise to the *formation of the Gay Liberation Front* (GLF) in the United States, which spread to much of Western Europe. The milestone of the modern homosexual movement came in 1969.

The *"Stonewall Uprising"* in New York was a response by homosexuals to police repression in the city's *"ghettos"* on June 28, 1969. The confrontation with the police began at dawn and lasted four nights. On the first anniversary of the confrontation, homosexuals from several American states marched through the streets of New York, demonstrating their willingness to fight for their rights. June 28th was established as *Gay Pride Day* and parades are held in various parts of the world today in reference to this date.

For analytical purposes, the homosexual movement in Brazil can be divided into three different periods. The first corresponds to the emergence and expansion of this movement during the period of political *"openness"* and has been recorded by most of the available bibliography on the subject.

At that time, the initiatives were very much concentrated on the Rio-Sao Paulo axis, were strongly marked by an anti-authoritarian and communitarian character, by a relapse into proposals for transforming society as a whole and were treated by the bibliography on social movements as part of the so-called *"alternative"* or *"libertarian"* movements.

This first period ended in the last years of the first half of the 1980s, which coincided with the return to democratic rule and the emergence of AIDS, then known as the *"gay plague".* The period that follows and comprises the remainder of the 1980s has been treated very little by the specific bibliography, and has been heralded as corresponding to a *"decline" of* the movement. Furthermore, analyses carried out in this context pointed to difficulties regarding the viability of a homosexual identity policy in Brazil.

In the early 1990s, the lack of bibliographical references on the continuity of this movement's activities in Brazil gave the impression that, in fact, the beginning of the 1980s had seen the apogee and end of a significant but short trajectory.

However, around the beginning of the 1990s, there was a revival of militant initiatives in 1995. It was possible to see that this movement had survived the process of *"re-democratization"*, the failure of its model of community and autonomist organization and the emergence of AIDS. What's more, it reached the second half of the 1990s with a strong presence in the media, extensive participation in human rights movements and in response to the AIDS epidemic, links to international networks and associations defending human rights and gay and lesbian rights, support for parliamentarians with the proposal of bills at federal, state and municipal level, and work with state agencies linked to STD/AIDS and human rights issues, formulating various responses to the exclusion of religious organizations, creating associations of groups/organizations at national and local level - such as the *Brazilian Association of Gays, Lesbians and Transvestites* or the *Forum Paulista de Gays, Lesbians, Bisexuals and Transgenders* - and the organization of street events, such as the demonstration held on the occasion of *Gay Pride* Day in the city of Sao Paulo, which, in 2002, was attended by an estimated 500,000 people.000 people.

The first homosexual group was created in 1978, called *"Somos"*. Years later, the non-governmental organization GGB - *Grupo Gay da Bahia* was founded, which, according to its research, showed that more than 190 homosexuals were murdered in Brazil in 2008. Unfortunately, violence is not only physical but also often moral, violating a person's integrity.

The role of the movements is precisely to ensure that new objectives are achieved, that debates on important issues do not cease. To do this, they can take on new forms in social spaces, increasing their visibility and seeking the establishment of real equality and universal access to public space. Political and social participation is a process that gives meaning and significance to a social movement, developing critical awareness and generating a new political culture.

3. BRIEF FAMILY HISTORY

Studying the history of humanity, one can see that the family entity is the first human expression of social organization, since the emergence of man, the family has existed, albeit involuntarily and naturally, with the basic functions of reproduction and defense of its members.

Some scholars, such as Cristiano Chaves de Farias, state that *"there is no doubt that the family, in the history of human groupings, is what precedes all others, as a biological and social phenomenon, which is why it needs to be understood from different angles"* (2007, p. 1).

According to historical accounts, it can be seen that since the dawn of civilization, human beings have come together to form families, forming so-called human groups in various forms and for various purposes.

Thus, according to Bittar (1989, p. 1), it is necessary to verify that man tends to get closer to his fellow human beings in order to satisfy his own, patrimonial or personal needs, binding himself through ideals, feelings and reciprocal interests.

The family institution is therefore older than the state, perhaps even than religion itself, and consequently predates the law. Along these lines of thought, says Euclides Oliveira:

> The first and main form of human grouping, the family preexists the very legal organization of life in society, which is why it gave rise to it, and is considered the *maternal* cell of a nation. Its formation derives primarily from the rules of natural law, not least because of the instinctive phenomenon of preserving and perpetuating the human species (2003, p. 23).

In this way, talking about the family and its origins means paying attention to the fact that it changes according to the time in which it is inserted, but this is a difficult task, according to Eduardo de Oliveira Leite (1994, p. 7), talks about the family before the existence of the Law, due to the lack of documents and material sources that portray its beginnings.

However, even with this difficulty, the family has always been the object of study for various sciences, and it couldn't be otherwise, because it is the foundation of society, portraying the relationships of citizens throughout each historical moment in which it originated.

It should also be noted that the family remains a condition for humanization, socialization and the matrix of society, even with the transformations and evolution that it has undergone over time (PETRINE, 2004, p. 47), since it is the family that is the cradle for the emergence of new ideas and idealizations, which change based on the new desires of its members.

Thus, due to the variety of factors that structure the family, it is imperative to understand it according to the movements that constitute social relations over time and cultural space.

Some theorists, Rodrigo da Cunha Pereira notwithstanding, believed that at a given moment in history, *"every woman belonged to every man and every man to every woman"* (2003, p. 15), in other words, there were no specific rules or laws governing the exclusive bonds between men and women.

Orlando Soares (1999, p. 3) does not disagree with this, stating that the ancient family was not an essential factor for human procreation, precisely because of the great period of promiscuity experienced in antiquity. However, this issue of promiscuity is very controversial, with Caio Mario da Silva Pereira (1997, p. 17) adhering to the doctrine against the promiscuity thesis, defending the simple existence of certain taboos and impediments, stating that exclusivity is an inherent characteristic of the human essence; in the same vein, Rodrigo da Cunha Pereira (1999, p. 21), stating that there is a relationship between the two. 21), stating that there was a different kind of kinship relationship to the one we see today, with a little more freedom, but which did not reach the level of promiscuity.

What can be seen, then, in the studies on promiscuity in the historical relationship of the family, is that there was greater freedom between people, but it did not reach the barbarity of promiscuity, because as Rodrigo da Cunha Pereira (2003, p. 16) concludes, from the beginning of civilization there were already some impediments and taboos, and there was not the promiscuity that many thinkers defended.

In this context, what can be observed is that the family has changed over the decades and has undergone important influences in each era. However, its obvious social importance remains unchanged, because the family is the first expression of feeling and interest between people, It is a condition for humanization, socialization and the matrix of society, even with the transformations and evolution that it undergoes over the course of the ages, because the family is a breeding ground for new emotions and idealizations, which change based on the new desires of its members (2004, p. 47). 47). In the clear words of anthropologist Cynthia A. Sarti, *"the family will be the concretization of a way of living the basic facts of life"* (2000, p. 40).

Therefore, due to the variety of factors that structure the family, it is imperative to understand it according to the movements that constitute social relations over time and cultural space.

In the contemporary (post-modern) world, the family no longer has a natural character, but has taken on a new form, now forged in cultural phenomena, which is why Rodrigo da Cunha Pereira rightly asserts that it is *"a psychic structure that enables human beings to establish themselves as subjects and develop relationships in the polis"* (2001, p. 35).

The law is concerned with protecting the family as a

constitutionally guaranteed value, mainly because the Universal Declaration of Human Rights recognized the human person's right to found a family and, under this scenario, its protection is established in a privileged way in view of its extremely important role in promoting human dignity (TEPEDINO, 2004, p. 372).

Therefore, new definitions have emerged for the family and for filiation, based on values such as love and solidarity, overcoming the codified regime that gave way to the constitutionalized family (FACHIN, 2003, p. 2).

And that the family phenomenon *"is not a homogeneous totality, but a universe of differentiated relationships"* (SARTI, 2000, p. 39), which affect each of the parties within it in a different way, consequently requiring a multidisciplinary approach for a global understanding.

Undoubtedly, the family has a biological, spiritual and social dimension, and it is therefore necessary to understand it from a broad perspective, considering its idiosyncrasies and peculiarities, which requires the participation of different branches of knowledge, such as sociology, psychology, anthropology, philosophy, theology, biology (and, likewise, biotechnology and bioethics) and also the science of law (FARIAS, 2015, p. 4). 4).

3.1. The Family in Roman Law

The family in Rome was founded on the principle of authority, since the *pater* was at the same time the political head, priest and judge, with the father having power over women and also the power of life and death over his children *(ius vitae ac necis),* as Marco Aurelio Viana (1998, p. 24) explains. From this perspective, it can be understood that in Rome the family was represented by the so-called *patria potestas*, who was the oldest living common ancestor, with the power of command over all his descendants regardless of the consanguineous line.

In line with the independence of the bloodline of the Roman family, Mauricio Luiz Mizrahi states that *"The members of the ancient Roman family did not necessarily have a blood tie between them. At least, this was not absolutely a determining element* (2001, p. 34).

The blood bond was not central to the Roman family because its composition extended to include slaves as well, as property of the *father*, like his wife and children.

Thus, to paraphrase Rodrigo da Cunha Pereira (2003, p. 62), the bond established in the Roman family was not established by blood, but by marriage, in which the wife, children, grandchildren, great-grandchildren and also the assets were subject to the power of the *pater.* Consequently, it can be said that the Roman state hardly interfered in the family, which was guided, commanded and administered by the eldest common ancestor, the so-called *pater familia.* According to Arnold Wald (2004, p. 2), the Roman family was an economic, religious, political and jurisdictional unit, since it encompassed a whole range of interests within a single institution, which was the family led by the *pater.*

According to Magalhaes (2002, p. 9), in Rome, in the period before Christ, unions had the characteristic of perpetuating themselves. However, this position changed with the birth of Christ, when marriage became an indissoluble and sacramental institution, with the central objective of subsistence and exploitation of a property or the maintenance of a social level.

In this way, it can be said that marriage at that time represented a political and economic link, not based on a bond of affection and love between its members (LEITE, 2001, p. 15), since marriage served as an incentive for unions between economically wealthier people, leaving non-marital unions, generally formed by the low-income population, on the margins of the family.

Continuing with this thought, it is important to note what Fustel de Coulanges says, explaining that marriage in Roman times was invested more with patrimonial aspects than the affective feeling between people, *in* other words, *"it could even exist in the depths of hearts, but it meant nothing"* (2006, p. 45).

It can be seen that the union between a man and a woman in Rome was based on the indissolubility of monogamous marriage, because it was only in this way that it generated effects in the legal world. However, although only effects were accepted in the Roman legal relationship generated precisely through marriage, as Pedrotti (1999, p. 1) explains; concubinage was still found, which formed a distinct relationship and *"inferior to marriage"*, because it did not ensure the same effects as *marriage*.

Reinforcing this thought, Medeiros (1997, p. 117) also believes that Roman concubinage was a quasi-marriage considered inferior to marriage, since it lacked the *affectio maritalis* and the social and family purpose always present in marriage. It should be noted, therefore, that the intention in keeping the family restricted to marriage, i.e., formed by and only by marriage, excluding any other form of union, was to guarantee the patrimonialization of the family, always seeking to defend the assets commanded by the *pater.*

In this way, the man was considered to be the authority of the Roman family, as he exercised command over the lives of all its members and also over its assets, thus visualizing the Roman family organization as being based exclusively on male authority, with women being placed on the margins of the family system.

This was a time, as we have already said, when women, children and property came to belong to and be managed by the husband, instilling in the family an expression of the *pater*'s power and arbitrariness, leaving all descendants and wives at the mercy of his will and decisions.

Observing Bernardo Castelo Branco, it can be seen that,

> over the course of several centuries, the concept of the patriarchal family was solidified, based on its Roman roots, represented in its essence by paternal power, as a result of which the role of head and master of the decisions of family society was attributed, not admitting any challenge (2006, p. 17).

In this context, history shows that women have always been inferior and in Rome, it was no different, since Roman women were already born under the stigma of male dependence, as Rodrigo da Cunha Pereira cites, *who "was the property of her father, who had the right to choose her husband and marry her to whomever he wished"* (2003, p. 625), remaining under the domination of someone, in this case her husband, chosen by her father or under the domination of her own father.

It should also be noted that the dependence and inferiority of women at this time was well expressed by Mauricio Luis Mizrahi, who stated that *"women should not govern themselves; during childhood they depended on their father (if they were born into a religious marriage), and during youth, after the sacred union, they depended on their husband"* (2001, p. 41).

Adopting this line of thinking, women could be seen as a thing, a property of men, because they were literally used to bear children and meet men's biological needs, treated for the most part as commodities for their fathers and husbands.

However, with the passage of time and the emergence of the Empire, the Roman family evolved in the sense of restricting the authority of the *pater, with* greater autonomy being given to women and children. As WALD states:

> In the Empire, the *gens* disappears and inheritance and maintenance rights are granted to cognates. The state limits the *pater*'s authority, allowing the *alieni juris* to appeal to the magistrate in the event of abuse by the *pater.* The sale of children by the father disappeared, and the father was only allowed to apply modica *castigatio* (moderate punishment) (2004, p. 2).

In this sense, as a result of the autonomy granted to women in the imperial era, divorces and adultery arose in the family and the Roman family began to crumble.

In Rodrigo da Cunha Pereira's opinion, this inclusion of women outside the home, helping with the family economy, was a landmark change in the formalist structure of the matrimonialized Roman family.

It therefore notes that,

> The conquest by women of a place as the "Subject of Desire" led to the ruin of the indissolubility of marriage, since it was the woman's subordinacy that sustained these marriages. Once she became a subject and was no longer subjected, this had repercussions on the legal system and made indissoluble marriage unviable (2006, p. 5; 148).

It should be noted, therefore, that by no longer being satisfied with family life alone, women have undeniably contributed to the unfeasibility of the hitherto patriarchal system.

This profoundly altered the Roman family to the extent that it no longer ensured that the husband had absolute power over his wife, and it can be concluded that it was through women's persistence and pride in contributing to the family economy, inserting themselves into the field of work and supporting the household (PEREIRA, 2000, p. 35), that the Roman family, which was founded on female submission, began to be restructured.

It should also be pointed out that the ancient Roman family had these patriarchal ideals, because their purpose was to precipitate the organization of society and the defence of property, which is why the family was founded on rigid and limited precepts.

With this in mind, Cristiano Chaves de Farias (2007, p. 4) observes that the old family was a concept based on the unity of production and assets, with little regard for affective ties, making it impossible to dissolve the marriage bond, as it would correspond to the disorganization of society itself.

It can be commented that, with the decline of patriarchy, a new ideological process of family began, linked in particular, in the words of Joao Paulo Cunha (2006, p. 5), to the development of modern individualism in the 19th century, in an immense desire for happiness.

It can be seen that this view has influenced the model of family constitution in various cultures for a long time, analyzing them initially and for many years, based on the pillars erected by Roman society, seeing the family as an institute focused on subordinacy, procreation and patrimonial defense; characteristics present in the Roman family.

In this respect, for all that has been said so far, the Roman organization is considered to be a fundamental milestone for understanding the family described in Brazilian legislation, and has greatly influenced the family model in various places. However, nowadays, like Eduardo dos Santos, it is understood that *"the type of patriarchal family of other eras is positively not that of the present day"* (1999, p. 20), since the current family is no longer composed along the hierarchical, patriarchal and patrimonial lines of the Roman family.

3.2. The Family in Canon Law

There were many changes in the family during this historical phase which, for some theorists, provided a mirror for various cultures influenced by the model of Christianity. It was with the canonization of marriage, which began around the 9th century, that the Catholic Church took upon itself the power to regulate all marriages, demanding that the blessing of marriage be administered by priests (MAGALHAES, 2002, p. 13). 13). From then on, after the birth of Christ, marriage came under the exclusive rule of the Catholic Church, making marriage an indissoluble sacrament, i.e. *"before it was based solely on marital authority, it became a sacrament of marriage",* as Rodrigo da Cunha Pereira (2003, p. 62) cites.

Soon, the celebration of marriage was elevated to a sacramental rite, symbolizing the union of Christ and the Church, considering only the blessing of marriage by Catholic dogmas, instituted by Jesus Christ (MEDEIROS, 1997, p. 20), thus expressing that once married, only death could separate the couple.

In this way, Cristiano Chaves de Farias has well understood,

> that the family environment, necessarily matrimonialized, was governed by the rule until death do us part, admitting the personal sacrifice of family members in the name of maintaining the bond of marriage. Thus, for Catholic doctrine, marriage was aimed at organizing society and protecting property, punishing those who dissolved the marriage with social exclusion, since the rule was that "what God has joined together, man cannot break" (2007, p. 4).

In this respect, it can be said that it was under the influence of Canon Law that the family came to be established almost exclusively by religious marriage, through a solemn celebration, sacramentalized in its indissolubility, and with the aim of reproduction, in other words, the sexual relationship between the couple was based solely on the biblical precept: *"grow and multiply"* (DIAS, 2004, p. 28), constituted for procreation and social organization.

It is worth mentioning here that the Church was the delineator of the family at this time, as it began to interfere decisively in family relations. However, it is worth noting that with Luther's Protestant Reformation, at the beginning of the Modern Age, positions contrary to this issue emerged, as Arnold Wald observes:

> For Protestants, competence in matters of family law belonged to the state and there was no justification for attributing a sacred character to marriage. Since it was a simple act of civil life, a natural contract, there was nothing to prevent the will of the spouses from dissolving the marriage bond, according to the reformed religion (2004, p. 15).

Thus, Catholics, disagreeing with this understanding, expressed their opinion through the Council of Trent, stating that marriage, besides having the character of a sacrament, could only be celebrated by the Church. Thus, Arnold Wald:

> As a reaction from Catholic circles, the Council of Trent (1542-1563) solemnly reaffirmed the sacramental nature of marriage, recognizing the exclusive competence of the Church and ecclesiastical authorities in everything related to marriage, its celebration and the declaration of its nullity (2004, p. 15).

In effect, reinforcing the model of canonical doctrine, those who were not married were left on the margins of society, and in this sense, Rosana Amara Girardi Fachin reports that, *"concubinage existed, but only among people on low incomes and clandestinely, not among the wealthy or middle classes, who through marriage guaranteed the transmission of property"* (2001, p. 35).

From this point on, it is possible to ascertain the importance of marriage for religion, since it is through marriage that property is protected, the driving force behind social and economic relations and the family at a time when the State and the Church were confused.

To paraphrase Fachin (2001, p. 36), marriage was then a kind of guarantee of respectability, security and ascension, as opposed to the ceremony of officially rejected concubine relationships.

Once these aspects have been singled out, it can be said that because of the influence of the Catholic Church, which defended monogamous marriage, many laws were passed in an attempt to prevent new family relationships from arising, with only the relationship between people through marriage being tolerated, thus also influencing the Brazilian Civil Code of 1916, since it accepted the processes of canon law, considering the matrimonial bond to be indissoluble (WALD, 2004, p. 21), making another family formation impossible in Brazilian law for a long time.

In this context, it can be seen that marriage was considered the sovereign family institution for a long time, although it is known that social reality is indifferent to what is laid down in law (VIANA, 1991, p. 22), because human feelings go beyond what can be laid down in law.

Thus, in the Christian era, concubinage was persecuted to the maximum, being cataloged as a sin and sanctions were created to curb such cohabitation. However, even with these initiatives against concubinage, severely combated by the Catholic Church, it did not cease to exist and has always been a social fact. Carmem Lucia Silveira Ramos adds:

> Therefore, the rejection of concubinage remained linked to the social discrimination suffered by the excluded. Furthermore, concubinage brought together couples from different social classes, a situation which, as in Rome, went against the prevailing marriage policy (2000, p. 62).

Thus, a broad link can be established between the prejudice impregnated in people's consciences, in accepting only what is common, the interest in protecting property, with the staunch exclusion of other forms of family, because although they have always existed in society, it was only marriage based on Catholic dogma that was socially accepted.

But, as Cristiano Chaves de Farias has said, *"the family is constantly changing as a result of the new conquests of humanity"* (2007, p. 4), and through these changes it can be seen that at the beginning of the 19th century, there was greater legislative concern with concubinage, helping, therefore, in the recognition of rights arising from this relationship.

And with the individualist and egalitarian philosophy of the French Revolution, the religious dogma regarding the family formed only by marriage was strongly contributed to (MEDEIROS, 1997, p. 33). Therefore, it is notable that when society began to accept personal relationships as sentimental unions, the legislator could no longer deny effects to these concubinage relationships, leaving them outside the law. Thus began the change in customs, the formation of an ideology focused on the human being and no longer on their assets, as occurred explicitly at a time when the Church had significant influence over society and the State itself.

Given this situation, it is important to note that understanding the past influence of Canon Law on Family Law is necessary in order to understand the contemporary family, as many aspects incorporated in the past of full influence of Catholic dogma are attributed to the current family.

3.3. The 19th century family: Post-modernity.

In the 19th century, the state invaded family life, legislating on marriage, regulating the adoption process, determining the rights of natural children, instituting divorce and limiting paternal power. It was the state that guaranteed individual rights and encouraged family and paternal unity (CENTA, 1999. p. 2).

The head of these families was the husband. As already mentioned, the wife and children had a lower position than him. In this way, the will of the family was translated into the will of the man, which became the will of the family entity. However, these powers were restricted to the matrimonialized family, the so-called illegitimate children had no place in the original codified family, only the legitimate ones were part of that productive family unit. Furthermore, the indissolubility of marriage was the rule, and the only way to resolve a marriage that hadn't worked out was divorce, which put an end to the communion of life, but not to the legal bond (DIAS, 2007, p. 30).

At the end of the 19th century, every mother took care of her baby, and this dedication to her children was even expressed in their education. She dedicated herself to this task while maintaining the child's social and sexual differences. As for the father, the Civil Code established the absolute superiority of the husband, who dominated both public and private space: he was the master of money and decision-making power (CENTA, 1999, p.16).

Fortunately, with social/family developments, legislative changes were inevitable, some of them very significant. One example is the Married Women's Statute (Law No. 4,121/1962), which gave women back their full capacity, as it guaranteed them ownership of property acquired through their work. Another piece of legislation was the Divorce Law (EC 9/1977 and Law 6.515/1977) which, as Maria Berenice DIAS points out: *"Ended the indissolubility of marriage, eliminating the idea of the family as a sacralized institution"* (2007, p. 30).

In the 20th century, at the same time as the State distanced itself from the Church, known as *secularization,* new phenomena emerged. The liberation of customs, the women's revolution, the result of the feminist movement and the emergence of contraceptive methods, and the evolution of genetics, which made new forms of reproduction possible, were all factors that contributed to resizing the concept of the family (SIQUEIRA, 2012, p. 8).

In the light of contemporary law, based on democratic principles of improvement and the dignity of the individual, enshrined in most modern constitutions, it is no longer possible to consider only the relationship between a man and a woman, anointed by the bonds of marriage, as a family. Thus, once the paradigms identifying the family, which were previously based on the marriage/sex/reproduction triad, have been broken, it is necessary to look for a new concept of family (SIQUEIRA, 2010, p. 1).

Today's family model is no longer one of authoritarianism, nor one that is formed by the institute of marriage, but one that is founded on bonds of affection.

The post-modern family is marked by affection between its members and the constant search for happiness. According to Pedro Belmiro Welter (2003, p. 31), from this historical moment onwards, the family opens up to become a cruel world, a form of shelter, a bit of human warmth, a home where solidarity, fraternity and, above all, bonds of affection and love are practiced among its members. This is the meaning of family today.

According to Eliane Goulart Martins Carossi, (2003, p. 55) the family began its transition to contemporaneity with the entry of women into the labor market around 1950 and the achievement of equality between spouses. With the discovery of the contraceptive pill in mid-1967, the family ceased to be an economic entity and marriage began to be based on love and no longer on an economic contract (DILL, 2012, p. 3).

Affection has become an essential element for the union between people, making them accomplices in love and happiness, thus forming diverse family entities, protected or not by law. Currently, there are families with children, without children, homosexual families, among others. *"Advances in science and technology have created new social expectations and new possibilities for family law, which has no alternative but to become aware of these new forms of social organization"* (ALDROVANDI, 2006, p. 6).

The contemporary family is characterized by diversity, justified by the incessant search for affection and happiness. In this sense, a new way of thinking about family law has emerged. In the words of Mara Berenice DIAS:

> A new name has emerged for this new tendency to identify the family by its affective involvement: the eudemonist family, which seeks individual happiness through the emancipation of its members (2007, p. 52).

According to the author:

> Eudemonism is the doctrine that emphasizes the subject's search for happiness. The absorption of the eudemonist principle into the legal system changes the meaning of the legal protection of the family, shifting it from the institution to the subject, as can be seen in the first part of §8 of article 226 of the Federal Constitution: the State will ensure assistance to the family in the person of each of its components (Ibidem.).

The new vision of family therefore affirms *"a relationship based on emotional communication, in which the rewards derived from such communication are the main basis for the continuation of the relationship"*, in Anthony Giddens' fine conception (2000, p. 70).

By calling the traditional family structure into question, contemporaneity (amid countless technological, scientific and cultural innovations) has made it possible to understand the family as a subjective organization that is fundamental to the individual construction of happiness. It is therefore necessary to recognize that in addition to the traditional family, based on marriage, other family arrangements fulfil the role that contemporary society has assigned to the family: an entity for the transmission of culture and the formation of a dignified human person.

The transition from the family as an economic unit to an egalitarian understanding aimed at promoting the development of its members' personalities reaffirms a new role, now based on affection.

4. EVOLUTION OF THE CONCEPT OF FAMILY IN THE BRAZILIAN LEGAL SYSTEM

The Civil Code does not define what family is, but in general civil law considers family to be people united by a marital or kinship relationship.

Arnold Wald (2004, p. 9-10) states that the Brazilian family suffered a great influence from the Roman family, which depended on consanguinity and was defined as the group of people who were under the *patria potestas of* the oldest living common ancestor.

There was a single estate belonging to the family, which was administered by the *pater.* With evolution, individual estates emerged, but they were managed by people who were under the authority of the *pater.*

The aforementioned author also argues that the family was simultaneously an economic, religious, political and jurisdictional unit. It had its own religion, usually the religion of deceased ancestors, and it was the *pater familia* who administered internal justice. The family was also considered a political unit because the Senate was made up of the heads of families (ibid.).

The basis of the family has not changed much over time, as it is still made up of parents and children, but today's family differs from the old ones in that it has undergone changes in composition and the role played by fathers and mothers.

In the past, while fathers worked to provide for their children, mothers were responsible for raising them. However, the family has undergone countless transformations throughout history. The biggest of these began with the industrial revolution, when women entered the labor market en masse and the male figure also began to collaborate in domestic work. With the revolution, the female figure became increasingly scarce, taking care exclusively of domestic chores and raising the children, while the husband had the obligation to provide for the household. Thus, the patriarchal family gave way to the modern family (PEREIRA, 2001).

In this sense, the notion of the family has undergone changes in terms of its structure. Considered to be the first social cell, the family institution has undergone several mutations and is currently continuing to adapt to a modern world that is becoming more and more dynamic every day due to social events resulting from changes in customs. Today it's possible to find family units that didn't used to exist and that question the model of the traditional Western family, i.e. the one formed by a father, mother and child.

Family models are becoming more diverse. Single-parent families are common, formed by a father or mother and their child; families formed only by siblings; cousins; uncles and nephews; grandparents and grandchildren and, why not, families formed by homosexuals, without children, with children of one of them or even with children adopted by one of them. As long as there is love and affection, these human formations deserve to be called a family, because they fulfill its function in their daily lives. In the face of so much diversity, it is difficult to conceptualize family. Nowadays, there are various types, but the concept and purpose are the same.

Socio-affective families, i.e. families formed by the affective bond and not just by the blood factor, are a reality today, and it cannot be said that there has been a trivialization of this institute, but rather a modernization that encompasses groups other than the traditional ones, but with the same objective.

With due legal support, its concept is based on the fact that the family institution exists from the moment it is based on the feeling between its components, and it understands that characteristics such as affection, living together with love, respect and mutual assistance should be emphasized in a relationship, even if it takes place on the margins of marriage. But these changes do not mean that prejudices have disappeared. On the contrary, they are still more and more present. There is still no acceptance of acts or behaviors that go beyond what is considered *"right"*.

When it comes to the family formed by same-sex unions, many judges still don't recognize essential rights such as freedom, equality and dignity, which are guaranteed by the Constitution. Few recognize it as a stable union.

The Constitution, in granting protection to the family, regardless of whether or not marriage has taken place, has established a new concept of family entity, embracing other affective bonds. But the constitutional wording is merely an example, expressly referring to the stable union between a man and a woman and the relationship of one of the ascendants with their offspring. *The caput of art. 226 is therefore a general clause of inclusion, and it is not admissible to exclude any entity that meets the requirements of affection, stability and ostensibility* (LOBO, 2002, p. 95).

The concept of family has become more pluralized and is no longer identified by the celebration of marriage. There is no way of affirming that art. 226, § 3, of the Federal Constitution, by mentioning the stable union formed between a man and a woman, recognized only this coexistence as worthy of protection by the State.

What exists is a simple recommendation to turn it into a marriage. At no point has it been said that there are no family entities formed by people of the same sex. To demand differentiation between the sexes in a couple in order to be protected by the state is to make a *"hateful distinction"* (SUANNES, 1999, p. 32), a clearly discriminatory stance that goes against the principle of equality, ignoring the existence of a ban on differentiating people on the basis of their sex.

No type of bond based on affection can be denied the *status* of a family, deserving of state protection, since the Federal Constitution (art. 1, III) enshrines respect for the dignity of the human person as a petrea norm (DIAS, 2005, p. 45).

5. HISTORY AND EVOLUTION OF ADOPTION

Adoption has had a very particular historical evolution, as it is one of the oldest institutes and part of the customs of almost all peoples, its concept varies according to the time and traditions of each people (GRANATO, 2010, p. 27). Therefore, it has different concepts and purposes at different times.

In ancient times, the institute of adoption was used as a way of perpetuating the domestic cult; religion was the most powerful bond between the members of a family. The meaning of adoption was linked to the perpetuity of the family, through religious worship, with filiation fulfilling the patrimonial, moral and religious continuity of the family (GIRARDI, 2005, p. 113). Personal desires were not fundamental, but religious worship was.

In this period, Silvio Rodrigues states that the last way to ensure the continuity of the family and the perpetuation of its cult, when there was no possibility of having a child, was through the institute of adoption, and it was up to the children to worship the memories of their ancestors (2004, p. 335). Those who were unable to do so risked having their family extinguished because they had no way of worshipping their ancestors. Adoption was seen as a way of giving continuity to domestic religion, through the continuity of funerary offerings and as a way of saving the home. Adoption was only allowed for those who had no children, and only as a means of preventing the extinction of a cult.

In Greece, adoption served a social and political purpose, where only citizens could adopt and be adopted (JUNIOR, 2008, p. 91). Venosa states that adoption was a means of maintaining the cult of the family through the male line, since the right of succession was only allowed to men. Therefore, the social, political and religious purpose of adoption, aimed at the interests of the adopter, was perceptible at that time.

> In Greek society, the fundamental characteristic of adoption was that the adoptee was completely cut off from the family of origin, not even being able to pay respects to the biological father, and there was a clear distinction between the adopted child and the natural child. The Greeks allowed both men and women to be adopted, although only men had the right to be adopters and only citizens could adopt and be adopted (2003, p. 253).

In Sparta, the state took young children for itself in order to prepare them for the military, and for this reason it is very difficult for the institute of adoption to have existed there.

In Rome, the institute of adoption had its greatest significance, following the transformations of the Roman family regarding adoption in the Roman phase, Granato expressed himself in this way:

> In addition to the need to perpetuate the domestic cult and give continuity to the family, adoption also served a political purpose, allowing plebeians to become patricians and vice versa, such as Tiberius and Nero, who were adopted by Augustus and Claudius and joined the tribunate (2010, p. 38).

Adoption already had its traces in the *Law of the XII Tables,* considered the oldest written Roman legislation.

In the Middle Ages, the institute declined significantly, because the Catholic Church saw adoption as a direct affront to its economic interests, since if someone didn't have children, they would leave their assets to the Church. However, if you had an adopted child, this process would be broken. Thus, the institute was not contemplated in Canon Law.

In the Modern Age, adoption arose again with the legislation of the French Revolution, and was later included in the Code of Napoleon (1804). On adoption in France, Wald taught very well:

> It was up to France to resurrect the institute, giving it new foundations and regulating it in the Code of Napoleon, at the beginning of the 19th century, in the interest of the Emperor himself, who was thinking of adopting one of his nephews. French law at the time only allowed adoption for adults, requiring the adopter to have reached the age of fifty, making adoption so complex and the rules so strict that it was of little use and rarely applied. Later laws lowered the age requirement and made adoption easier, allowing it to better develop its role in modern society (1999, p. 188).

Finally, it is worth mentioning the institute of adoption in Portuguese law, which greatly influenced the institute in Brazil. In that country, with adoption, the adopter did not acquire patrio poder and as for succession, the prince had to authorize it in order for the adoptee to be entitled to succession.

In this way, adoption in Portugal functioned as a form of requesting maintenance and only acquired the characteristics of Roman law with the consent of the Prince.

5.1. Adoption in Brazil

Adoption was introduced in Brazil under the *Philippine Ordinances* and the first law to deal with the subject, in an unordered way, was enacted on September 22, 1828, with characteristics of Portuguese law, originating from Roman law. During this period, the procedure for adoption was judicialized and, consequently, it was the duty of the judges of the first instance to confirm the wishes of the interested parties in a hearing, where the letter of adoption was issued. This was followed by other provisions that also dealt with the institute, such as Decree No. 181 of January 24, 1890, the Consolidation of *Civil Laws by Teixeira Freitas* and the *New Consolidation of Civil Laws by Carlos de Carvalho,* published in 1915. But it was the *Civil Code of 1916* that was *the* first Brazilian law to systematically regulate the institute of adoption.

What is important is that, whether it is based on the *Civil Code,* the *Statute of the Child and Adolescent* - ECA, or both, adoption fulfills a considerable social function and must be understood without prejudice.

Adoption, as you can see, is an institute that has undergone changes over time, from a selfish attitude aimed only at guaranteeing family worship, and later property, to an act of love and solidarity. The main reason for adopting minors today is to protect children and teenagers, guaranteeing them a home, education, affection and, above all, a future.

Same-sex adoption is not regulated in Brazil, but it has been happening all over the country. However, prejudice and the lack of specific legislation have hindered this process. Homosexuals, like heterosexuals, have rights and duties, and are not exempt from fulfilling their duties because they have a different sexuality to the majority, but sexuality is a determining factor in fulfilling their rights.

The institute of adoption is dealt with by the *Child and Adolescent Statute* (ECA) in articles 39 to 52. Among the requirements listed for adoption, none refers to the sexual orientation of the adopter. Due to the absence of any legal restriction, it is possible for homosexuals to adopt, as it is clear that the minor will be in accordance with Article 43 of the ECA:

> Art. 43: Adoption will be granted when it presents real advantages for the adoptee and is based on legitimate reasons.

This article states that the adoptee will be better supported in the bosom of a family than relegated to his or her own fate. The reasons are considered legitimate when the adopter's intentions, wrapped up in feelings arising from the parental relationship, are in harmony with the purpose of the institute to achieve the well-being of the minor.

As Silva Junior points out:

> The important thing is that, whether it is covered by the Civil Code, the Statute of the Child and Adolescent or both, adoption has a considerable social function today; it must be understood beyond the prejudiced heritage (which has always permeated it) and therefore needs to be contextualized with the value-legal preponderance of affection and with the guiding constitutional principles of modern Family Law (2010, p. 109).

Article 42 of *the Child and Adolescent Statute* allows for adoption by people regardless of their sexual preferences, on the condition that the adopter is over 18 (eighteen) years old, regardless of marital status (wording given by Law No. 12.010 of 2009). In this way, adoption could be done by a single homosexual, as long as he met the requirements set out in the ECA. Article 227 of the *Federal Constitution* (CF/88) and Article 19 of the ECA guarantee children and adolescents the right to family life. Therefore, when it is not possible to keep them in their biological family, these minors should be given the opportunity to have a substitute family, placing them in adoptive homes and the sexual oppositions of their future parents should not be an obstacle.

6. PSYCHOLOGICAL EFFECTS OF SAME-SEX ADOPTION ON THE ADOPTEE

Always, when topics as grand as this one - *"adoption of children by same-sex couples"* - are debated, discriminatory illusions that have been blown up in the memory stubbornly rise to the surface. This is what part of the doctrine and jurisprudence has done, with astonishing ease, when debating the subject. To this end, they put forward propositions such as these:

> [In the case of two homosexuals who live together,] although there is no legal impediment, we believe that this adoption should not be possible, because the adoptee would have a distorted reference to the role of father and mother, as well as social problems of coexistence due to prejudice, condemnation and reprisal by third parties, entailing a risk to the psychological well-being of the adoptee that cannot be ignored (BRITO, 2000, p. 55).

Arnaldo Marmitt also believes that homosexual couples are *"contraindicated"* to adopt, and states that:

> The good reputation of the adopter is a point in their favor, and a prerequisite for a successful adoption [...] If on the one hand there is no impediment against the impotent, the same does not apply to transvestites, homosexuals, lesbians, sadists, etc. without sufficient moral conditions. Inconvenience and prohibition are more in line with the moral, natural and educational aspect (MARMITT, 1993, p. 111-13).

Debora Vanessa Caus Brandao also believes that it is impossible for homosexual couples to adopt, using as an argument the possibility of psychological upheaval for the child as a result of being raised by homosexuals. She adds:

> First and foremost, it is important to explore the psychological aspects of the subject, since partners, no matter how closely they relate under the same roof, cannot imitate human nature as man and woman, in the roles of father and mother (BRANDAO, 2002, p. 91).

As you can see, the most common question regarding adoption by a same-sex couple stems from the false idea that they are promiscuous relationships which do not offer a healthy environment for the proper development of a child. It is also alleged that the lack of behavioral references can lead to psychological sequelae and difficulties in the child's sexual identification.

In an attempt for science to present the development of personality and the influence of the environment on children's behavior, with regard to their sexual role and affective identity, many theories can be brought up, including Social Learning, Cognitive Development, Gender Schema and Psychoanalysis.

Historically, studies in developmental psychology have gone in two directions: one analyzing the influence of the adult on the developing child and, later, the influence of the child on the adult. The first of these lines of study was concerned with child rearing practices and the personality traits of the parents associated with the development of the child's personality (FALCAO, 2004. Postgraduate Program (Master's Degree in Psychology) - Universidade Catolica de Goias Vice-Rectory for Postgraduate Studies and Research).

Freud's (1856-1939) discoveries around the beginning of the 20th century brought new insights into imprecise and invisible human phenomena, through the study of dreams, acts of failure, emotions (study of hysteria) and sexuality.

They believed that the fetus and the newborn child, up to the age of 2 or 3, did not experience emotions, considering that the personality had not developed enough for any kind of relationship with the world. Freud (1856-1939) discovered the existence of sexual fantasies in childhood, but a fantasized sexuality around the family group. The triangular Oedipal configuration (e.g. mother, father and baby) will provide the basic organization for adult sexuality.

The importance of Freud's theorizing lies in *denaturalizing* human sexuality, demonstrating that all sexual choices, as productions of desire, also follow unconscious determinations, and that there is no such thing as normal, natural sexuality.

For Freud, homosexual behavior (or inversion) can date back to the beginning of the individual's existence, as far back as his memory can reach, or it can manifest itself shortly before or after puberty. It can persist throughout life or disappear temporarily, or it can be an isolated episode in the process of normal development. It can even appear for the first time late in life, after a long period of normal sexual activity, or after the individual has had a painful experience with the object of the opposite sex.

A different but equally important concept is that of Piaget (18941980), whose concern was to study thought processes from infancy to adulthood. Piaget (1894-1980) presented an interactionist vision, in which the child and the human being were in an act of continuous interaction with the environment. Therefore, the child will build mental structures and acquire ways of functioning in order to understand the world around them.

For this scholar, the child's way of thinking and learning goes through stages, showing the importance of gender constancy so that the child feels *"motivated to learn to behave in the expected or appropriate way for that gender"* (BEE, 1996, p. 304).

According to Piaget (1961), it is through schemas and representations that children come into contact with the environment. He emphasizes the role of direct reinforcement and influence in shaping children's sex role attitudes. It is thanks to schemas that we can interpret and give meaning to the environment, making it possible to grasp it.

Piaget (1961) states that affect plays an essential role in the functioning of intelligence. Without affect there would be no interest, no need, no motivation; and consequently, questions or problems would never be asked and there would be no intelligence.

Ricketts and Achtenberg (1989) proved that mental health and individual happiness depend on the dynamics of the family and not on the way it is structured. Patterson (1997) researched the influence of homosexual fathers and mothers on the sexual identity, personal development and relationships of adopted and biological children; his results show that both the level of adjustment of the maternal function and the self-esteem and social and personal development of these children are comparable to those of children raised by heterosexual couples; he also demonstrated that same-sex parents are potentially as affectionate as heterosexual parents.

According to Golobomk and Tasker (1996), constructivist theories, contemporary with Piaget, state that sexual feelings are not born with the individual or socialized by childhood experiences. They consider that sexual identity is constructed throughout life, as the individual develops their internal sexual fantasies according to the sexual stimulation they receive.

Finally, there is *Social Learning Theory* (Bandura, 1969), influenced by behaviorist theory, in which, according to Davis (1981), behavior is learned and modified by reinforcement variables that the subject comes into contact with through observation. The presence of stimuli (reinforcers) and incentives seems to act mainly as a facilitator of learning.

Indeed, Britzman points out that:

> "sexual identity is constantly being rearranged, destabilized and undone by the complexities of experience". In this respect, it becomes clearer that the parents' behavior and affection do not interfere in the basic constitution of their sexual orientation (...) as a psychic structural reality and a complex of uninterrupted desires, since this psychological rag depends on the combination of factors that have not yet been fully explained scientifically, among which the intersubjective dynamics of the parents-educators can only be presented as one of the summative causes (JUNIOR, 2005, p. 95).

Davis (1981) points out that, according to this approach, a large part of human learning depends on perceptual and cognitive processes, such as the distinct features of a given event and the observation of the physical and social environment.

Social Learning Theory emphasizes the role of direct reinforcement and influence in shaping children's sex role attitudes.

> This process would be verified through the construction of precise conceptions of gender in children, in other words, the building up of feelings that would lead them to identify more with the masculine or the feminine (JUNIOR, Enezio de Deus Silva, 2005, p. 96).

Behavior depends on *"the internal symbolic world, the ability to predict the consequences of behavior and a self-regulatory system that includes a self-rewarding system and a self-punishing system"* (ROSA, 2003, p.72).

For *Gender Schema Theory,* the understanding of gender begins to develop in children as soon as they perceive the behavioral differences between men and women.

The problem with adopting children lies in the idea that the upbringing given by the parents will determine the identity of the children. From this perspective, it is very likely that, in people's imaginations, adopters who do not fit into the socially established norms are undesirable as parents.

Psychological science has developed theories that naturalize certain forms of social relationships, marginalizing those relationships that don't fit into the forms considered *"natural".*

FINAL CONSIDERATIONS

From this research project, it can be seen that social movements are increasingly producing modernization, stimulating innovation and driving not only political reform, because the influence of such movements goes far beyond the political effects they produce; their support determines changes in behavior and rules on the part of individuals. The aim of these movements is not just equal rights, but the right to be different.

Based on this right to be different, citizens and societies today have combined the grammar of gender equality, ecological concerns, environmental conservation and the rights of the unborn, which were unthinkable before the emergence of social movements with these new agendas. And why not talk about the adoption of children by same-sex couples?

In view of the true metamorphosis undergone by the institute of adoption, which went from a selfish attitude aimed only at guaranteeing family worship, and later property, to an act of love and solidarity. The family itself has undergone major changes throughout history, with the emergence of other family models. The patriarchal family model has diminished in expression, and today it is no longer possible to say exactly which family model is the right one.

As Joao Baptista Villela (1979) says, the family has ceased to be a unit of economic, social and religious character and has become fundamentally a group of affection and companionship, which has given considerable reinforcement to the biological emptying of paternity, and it is imperative to question parental bonds in family structures formed by people of the same sex.

We can't close our eyes and try to believe that homoparental families, because they don't have reproductive capacity, simply don't have children. We are faced with an increasingly present reality: children and teenagers live in homosexual homes. Gays and lesbians are trying to fulfill their dream of forming a family with the presence of children. Not seeing this truth is using the mechanism of invisibility to deny rights, a discriminatory stance with a distinctly punitive character, which only generates injustice.

Just as divorce caused a stir and took time to be assimilated by society, adoption by homosexual couples also causes controversy, strangeness and the most varied reactions possible in common sense. The most crucial question that arises is: *if a homosexual adopts a child, will that child become a homosexual?; what about the parental references of man and woman for these children?*

Existing studies do not justify the idea that children can become homosexual because they live with homosexuals, otherwise there would be no homosexuals in families that are actually made up of heterosexuals.

Regarding the importance of parental references for children adopted by a same-sex couple, experts in the field of psychology understand that children naturally choose a person close to them in their family circle and of the opposite sex to their caregiver. This parental figure can be represented by a grandmother, aunt, grandfather, cousin, etc. It's important for children to have role models of both sexes in their lives, but parents don't necessarily have to be of different sexes.

It is worth remembering that society is constantly changing, it is not a static reality, and the family is increasingly presenting different forms of organization, so to remain oblivious to this process would be to deny the indisputable, and the law would not achieve its goal: justice.

Not recognizing affective paternity as paternity could be a step backwards in the Brazilian legal system, given the transformations that are taking place in the legal world. Several judgments are already favoring socio-affective paternity in certain cases: voluntary recognition, adoption, Brazilian adoption and child rearing, but it is still resistant when it mentions affective paternity, without formalities such as in the judicial process, registration or notary's office, based only on possession of the state of being a child.

Legislators are intimidated when it comes to guaranteeing the rights of minorities excluded from power. The omission of the law makes it difficult to recognize rights, especially in situations that deviate from certain conventional standards, which increases the responsibility of the judiciary.

Prejudice and personal positions cannot lead the judge to use his sentence as a means of punishing behavior that deviates from the standards he accepts as normal. Likewise, the silence of the law cannot be invoked to deny rights to those who have chosen to live outside the standards imposed by conservative morality, but who do not harm the social order. Diversity needs to be respected. Exclusion and prejudice can no longer be tolerated.

Justice is neither blind nor deaf. Nor can it be mute. It needs to have its eyes open to see social reality, its ears attentive to hear the cries of those who are waiting for it and the courage to speak the law in consonance with justice.

REFERENCES

AIDAR, Adriana Marques.AIDAR, Maria Aura Marques. BARROS, Jaqueline de Melo. SANTOS, Fabio Fraga dos. SANTOS, Letfcia Lucia Silva. **Sexual orientation and identity in the constitution of social movements. Sem. de Saude do Trabalhador de Franca Sep. 2010. Available at:** <http://www.proceedings.scielo.br/scielo.php?pid=MSC000000011201000010 0033&script=sciarttext>. Accessed on: September 18, 2012.

ALDROVANDI, Andrea; SIMIONI, Rafael Lazzarotto. **Family law in the context of socio-affective organizations: Dynamics, Instability and Polyfamiliarity.** Brazilian Journal of Family Law. Porto Alegre, v. 7, n. 34, feb-mar. 2006.

ALEXANDRE, Gissele. **Adoption in Homosexual Relationships in Brazilian Law**. Monograph presented at the conclusion of the Graduation Course at the University of Vale do ItajatfSC . 2008. Available at: <http://siaibib01.univali.br/pdf/Giselle%20Alexandre.pdf>. Accessed on: 10 December 2012.

ALMEIDA, Marina S. Rodrigues Almeida. **The Prehistory of Children's Emotional Development.** Available at:<http://www.profala.com/artpsico24.htm>. Accessed on: September 18, 2012.

ALVAREZ, Larissa. **Adoption by gay couples.** Available at: <http://vilamulher.terra>. Accessed on: September 18, 2012.

AMAZONAS, Norma de Campos. **Adoption in Homosexual Relationships and the Process of Sexual Identification in Adoptees: a Literature Review**. Monograph presented at the conclusion of the Graduation Course UNORP - Centro Universitario do Norte Paulista de Sao Jose do RioPreto/SP . 2009. Available at : <http://www.aasptjsp.org.br/sites/default/files/Monografia-UNORP.pdf>. Accessed on: October 3, 2013.

ANDRADE, Rosiane de; Boeckel, Mariana Gonqalves. **Homosexual adoption: a study on the perception of institutionalized children.** Available at: <https://psicologia.faccat>. Accessed on: January 5, 2013.

ATAIDE, Marlene Almeida de. **Homosexual Social Movements in History: a question under analysis.** Seminario Internacional Enlaqando Sexualidades May 15-17, 2013 Universidade do Estado da Bahia, CampusISalvador/BA . Disponivelem:<http://www.uneb.br/enlacandosexualidades/files/2013/06/Os-

movimentossociais-dos-homossexuais-na-hist%C3%B3ria-uma-quest%C3%A3o-em-an%C3%A1lise.pdf>. Accessed on: December 10, 2012.

AZEVEDO, Daviane Aparecida de. **Social Movements, Civil Society and Social Transformation in Brazil**. Revista Multidisciplinar da Uniesp.SaberAcademico,n.09,iun.2010.Diponivelem:<http://bibliodigital.uniiui.edu.br:8080/xmlui/bitstream/handle/123456789/2773/MONOGRAFIA%20WILSON%20LUIZ%20PIMMEL.pdf?sequence=1>. Accessed on: September 2 012.

AZEVEDO,R.**Homosexualismo.**Disponivelem:<http://blig.ig.com.br/otroglodita/tag/homossexualismo.>. Accessed on: September 18, 2012.

BEE, Helen. **The developing child**. Porto Alegre: Artes Medicas, 1996

BITTAR, Carlos Alberto. **Family Law**. 2.ed.Rio de Janeiro: Forense Universitaria, 2006.

BRANDAO, Debora Vanessa Caus. **Homosexual partnerships**: legal aspects. Sao Paulo: Revista dos Tribunais, 2002.

BRITO, Kalyne Lopes de. **Adoption of children and adolescents by homosexual couples as a result of the expansion of the list of constitutionalized family entities based on the principle of equality.** Revista da Esmesc, v. 15, n. 21, 2008.

BRITZMAN, Deborah P. **What is this thing called love? Homosexual identity, education and curriculum**. In: Revista & Realidade. Porto Alegre, n. 21 (1), jan/jun. 1996.

CANALI, Elenice Buda; Miranda, Fernando Silveira. **Homosexual Unions: Some Sociological, Psychological and Legal Aspects.** Available at: <http://www.facsaoroque>. Accessed on: May 11, 2013.

CAROSSI, Eliane Goulart Martins**. Family relations and family law in the 21st century.**Revista Faculdade de Direito, Caxias do Sul. v. 12,2003.

CENTA, Maria deLourdes ; ELSEN, Ingrid. **Reflection on the evolution history of the family. Familia, Saude e Desenvolvimento**, v. 1, n. 1, 1999.

CENTA, Maria deLourdes ; ELSEN, Ingrid. **Reflection on the evolution family history. Family, Health and Development**. Family, Health

Desen. Curitiba, v.1, n.1/2, p.15-20, jan./dez. 1999. 15. Available at: <https://www.google.com.br/url?sa=t&rct=j&q=&esrc=s&source=web&cd=1&cad=rja&uact=8&ved=0ahUKEwjeoey6dfPAhXCHx4KHVtODa0QFggcMAA&url

=http%3A%2F%2Frevistas.ufpr.br%2Frefased%2Farticle%2Fdownload%2F4878%2F3728&usg=AFQjCNEYm9xOGqitlOq9f8rCockX BPQqQ&bvm=bv.135475266,d.Y2I>. Accessed on: May 11, 2013.

CORREIA, Joao Carlos. **Communication and Citizenship: the Media and Identities in Pluralist Societies.** Lisbon, Livros Horizonte. 2004. Available at:<https://www.researchgate.net/publication/263162622 ComunicaçãooeCidadaniaosmedia eafragmentacaodo espacespubliconassociedades pluralistas Lisboa Livros Horizonte 2004>. Accessed on: September 18, 2012.

COSTA, Aline Grigoletti de Lacerda. **Legal aspects of adoption by homosexuals.** Available at: <http://www.unibrasil>. Accessed on: May 11, 2013.

COSTA, Aline Grigoletti de Lacerda. **Legal aspects of adoption by homosexuals.**Available at:<http://www.unibrasil.com.br/arquivos/direito/20092/aline-grigoletti-de-lacerda-costa.pdf>. Accessed on: May 11, 2013.

CUNHA, Ana Mayara Oliveira. **Adoption by same-sex couples: From prejudice to the Principle of the Dignity of the Human Person.** Available at: <http://www.ambito-juridico>. Accessed on: December 12, 2012.

CUNHA, Ana Mayara Oliveira. **Adoption by same-sex couples: From prejudice to the Principle of the Dignity of the Human Person.** Available at:<http://www.viajus.com.br/viajus.php?pagina=artigos&id=2954&idAreaSel=2&seeArt=yes>. Accessed: December 18, 2012.

CUNHA, Tainara Mendes. **The historical evolution of the adoption institute**. Available at: <http://www.conteudojuridico>. Accessed on: September 12, 2012.

CUNHA, Tainara Mendes. **The historical evolution of adoption**. Available at: <http://www.conteudojuridico.com.br/artigo,a-evolucao-historica-do-instituto-da-adocao,34641.html>. Accessed on: September 12, 2012.

DIAS, Maria Berenice. **Homosexual adoption.** Available at: <http://www.mariaberenice>. Accessed on: January 5, 2013.

DIAS, Maria Berenice. **Homosexual unions in the face of the Federal Constitution.**

Available at:<http://www.mariaberenice.com.br/uploads/as uni%F5es hom

oafetivas frentea constitui%E7%E3ofederal - i.pdf>. Accessed on: 12 December 2012.

DIAS, Maria Berenice. **Conversando sobre homoafetividade**. Porto Alegre: Livraria do Advogado, 2004.

DIAS, MariaBerenice . **Homoaffective family**. Available at : <http://www.mariaberenice>. Accessed on:December 12, 2012.

DIAS, MariaBerenice . **Homoaffective family**. Available at : <http://www.cchla.ufrn.br/bagoas/v02n03art02 dias.pdf>. Accessed on:December 12, 2012.

DIAS, Maria Berenice. **Family Law Manual**. 4. ed. Sao Paulo: RT, 2007.

DIAS, Maria Berenice. **Homoparental Paternity**. Available at: <http://www.investidura.com.br/biblioteca-juridica/artigos/113-direito-constitucional/2314>. Accessed on: October 5, 2013.

DIAS, Maria Berenice. **Uniao homoafetiva: O preconceito & a justipa**. 4 ed. Porto Alegre: Livraria do Advogado Ed., 2009.

DIAS, Maria Berenice. **Homosexual union, prejudice and justice**. 3. ed. Porto Alegre: Livraria do Advogado, 2005.

DIAS, Maria Berenice. **Homosexual union: social and legal aspects**. In: Revista Brasileira de Direito de Familia, a. I, n. 4, jan./feb./mar. , 2000. Porto Alegre: Sintese.

DILL, Michele Amaral. CALDERAN, Thanabi Bellenzier. **Historical and legislative evolution of family and stepfamily** . Available at em:<http://www.ambitojuridico.com.br/site/index.php?nlink=revistaartigos leitura&artigo id=9019>. Accessed on: November 10, 2012.

Dill, Michele Amaral; Calderan, Thanabi Bellenzier. **Historical and legislative evolution of family and filiation.** Available at: <http://www.ambito-juridico.com.br>. Accessed on: November 25, 2012.

FACCHINI, R. **Sopa de letrinhas?** Rio de Janeiro: Garamond, 2005.

FACCHINI, Regina. **Movimento Homossexual no Brasil: recompondo um historico**. Cad. AEL, v.10, n.18/19, 2003. Disponivel at:<http://www.al.sp.gov.br/repositorio/bibliotecaDigital/20788 arquivo.pdf>. Accessed on: November 2012.

FACHIN Luiz Edson. **Direito de familia: elementos criticos a luz do novo**

codigo civil brasileiro. 2ª . ed. Rio de Janeiro: Renovar, 2003. p. 2.

FALCAO, Luciene Campos. **Adoption of Children by Homosexuals: Beliefs and Forms of Prejudice.** Dissertation presented at the conclusion of the Postgraduate Course at the Psychology Department of the Catholic University of Goias, Goiás, GO , 2004 . Available at:<http://tede2.pucgoias.edu.br:8080/bitstream/tede/1931/1/Luciene%20Campos%20Falcao.pdf>. Accessed on: May 8, 2013.

FARIAS, Cristiano Chaves de. **The post-modern family: in search of lost dignity**. Available at: <http://www.revistapersona.com.ar/Persona09/9farias.htm>. Accessed on: December 2012.

FARIAS, Cristiano Chaves de. ROSENVALD, Nelson. **Civil Law Course. Families**. 7th ed. Vol. 6. Sao Paulo: Atlas. 2015. p.4.

FERREIRA, Daniel Rogers de Souza. **Ousar Dizer o Nome Movimento Homossexual e o Surgimento do GRAB no Ceara**. Monograph presented at the conclusion of the Graduation Course at the State University of Ceara/Fortaleza.2003.Available at:<http://www.uece.br/labvida/dmdocuments/ouzardizero nome.pdf>. Accessed on:12 December 2012.

FIGUEIREDO, L. C. de B. **Adoption for homosexuals**. 4. ed. Curitiba: Jurua, 2 004.

FRANQA, Maria Regina Castanho. **Homoaffective families.** Rev. bras. Psicodrama vol.17 no.1 Sao Paulo 2009. THEMATIC SEQUENCE: The family in post-modern society: the psychodramatic approach. Available at: <http://pepsic.bvsalud.org/scielo.php?script=sciarttext&pid=S0104-53932009000100003>. Accessed on: May 5, 2013.

FUTINO, Regina Silva; Martins, Simone; **Adoption by homosexuals - a new family configuration from the perspective of psychology and the law.** Available at: <http://pepsic.bvsalud.org/scielo>. Accessed on: January 25 2 013.

GIDDENS, Anthony. **World out of control: what globalization is doing to us.** Rio de Janeiro: Record. 2000.

GIRARD, V. **Contemporary families, filiation and affection.** The legal possibility of adoption by homosexuals. Porto Alegre: Livraria do Advogado, 2 005.

LIMA, Fabiana Cristovam. **Adoption of Minors by Homosexual Couples: legal possibility.** Available at: <http://www.conteudojuridico>. Accessed on: May 11, 2013.

LIMA, Fabiana Cristovam. **Adoption of Minors by Homosexual Couples: Legal Possibility.** Monograph presented at the conclusion of the Graduation Course at the Porto Velho Higher Education Institute/RQ.2009. Available at :<http://www.conteudojuridico.com.br/pdf/cj026395.pdf>. Accessed on: May 11, 2013.

MAGNQ, Thierrie. **Freud's Letter to the Mother of a Homosexual**. Available at: <http://thierriemagno.blogspot.com.br/2013/07/carta-de-freud-mae-de-um-homossexual.html>. Accessed on: September 18, 2012.

MARIANQ, Ana Beatriz Parana. **The Changes in the Traditional Family Model and Affection as a Pillar of Support for these New Family Entities**. at:<http://www.unibrasil.com.br/arquivos/direito/20092/ana-beatriz-parana-mariano.pdf>. Accessed on: May 11, 2013.

MARMITT, Arnaldo. **Adogao.** Rio de Janeiro: Aide, 1993.

MELLQ, Paula Lima Vaz de**. The Possibility of Homosexual Adoption in the Brazilian Legal System.** Escola da Magistratura do Estado do Rio de Janeiro.2010.Available at:<http://www.emerj.tjrj.jus.br/paginas/trabalhos conclusao/1semestre2010/trabalhos 12010/paulamello.pdf>. Accessed on: May 11, 2013.

MENEZES, Larissa Pacheco de. **Historical evolution of the family**. 2008. Make it available : <http://www.viajus.com.br/viajus.php?pagina=artigos&id=1708>. Accessed on November 11, 2012.

MENEZES, Larissa Pacheco de. **Historical evolution of the family.** Available at: <http://www.viajus>. Accessed on: September 18, 2012.

PEREIRA, Claudia de Moraes Martins Pereira. **Shared custody**. Monograph presented at the conclusion of the Post-Graduation Course at the Candido Mendes University/RJ. 2001.

PEREIRA, Rodrigo da Cunha. **Sexuality as seen by the courts**. 2. ed. Belo Horizonte: Del Rey, 2001.p.35.

PEREIRRA, Claudia de Moraes Martins. **An Approach to the Sharing of Assets and Adoption in Relationships** Monograph presented at the conclusion of the Postgraduate Course at the Recife Law School / Center for

Legal Sciences of the Federal University of Pernambuco / Ceara 2005.Available at: <http://repositorio.ufpe.br/bitstream/handle/123456789/4217/arquivo51191.pdf?sequence=1&isAllowed=y>. Accessed on: May 5, 2013.

PETRINI, Joao Carlos. *In:* FARIAS, Cristiano Chaves. **Current Issues in Family Law and Procedure**. Rio de Janeiro: Lumen Juris, 2004.

PIAGET, Jean. **Affectivity and Intelligence**. Available at: <httDs://www.ufrqs.br/Dsicoeduc/Diaqet/afetividade-e-inteliqencia/>. Accessed on: May 5, 2013.

POPPE, Laila Leticia Falcao. **New Legal and Social Formations of the Family and Affection as a Means of Effecting this Fundamental Right**. Dissertation presented at the conclusion of the Postgraduate Course at the Regional University of the Northwest of the State of Rio Grande do Sul/RS.2014. Available at:<http://bibliodigital.unijui.edu.br:8080/xmlui/bitstream/handle/123456789/2793/Laila%20Leticia%20Falc%C3%A3o%20Poppe.pdf?sequence=1>. Accessed on: December 10, 2015.

PRATA, Mirela Fernandes Celestino. **The Juridicity of Homosexual Relationships in the Brazilian Legal System**. Dissertation presented at the conclusion of the Master's Course at the Pontifical Catholic University of São Paulo/SP.2010.Available at:<http://www.dominiopublico.gov.br/download/teste/arqs/cp148769.pdf>. Accessed on: January 5, 2013.

RODRIGUES, Paulo de Tharso Brondi de Paula. **Adoption by Homosexual Couples: a critique of prejudice .** Available at at:<http://intertemas.unitoledo.br/revista/index.php/ETIC/article/viewFile/1726/1641>. Accessed on: December 11, 2012.

ROSA, Jorge et al. **Psychology and education: the meaning of learning**. Porto Alegre; Edipucrs, 2003.

SAKAGUCHI, W. M. O; BERTOCINI, C. **Homoparental Adoption**. Law Course - Faculdades Integradas de Ourinhos-FIO.

SANTIAGO, Rafael da Silva. **Contemporary Family Law: constitutionalized family entity**. Interfaces Cientificas - Direito Aracaju, V.1, N.21 , p. 57-66, feb.2013. Available at:<https://periodicos.set.edu.br/index.php/direito/article/viewFile/415/225>. Accessed on: May 5, 2013.

SARTI, Cynthia A. **Family and individuality: a modern problem**. *In:* CARVALHO, Maria do Carmo Brant de (Org.). A familia contemporanea em debate. Sao Paulo: Cortez, 2000.

SARTI, Cynthia A. **Family and individuality: a modern problem**. In: CARVALHO, Maria do Carmo Brant de (Org.). A familia contemporanea em debate. Sao Paulo: Cortez, 2000.

SILVA JUNIOR, Enezio de Deus. **The legal possibility of adoption by homosexual couples**. 4ª ed. Curitiba: Jurua Editora, 2010.

SILVA, Keith Diana da. **Family in Brazilian Civil Law**. Rev. Npi/Fmr. Sep. 2010. Available at:<http://www.fmr.edu.br/npi/045.pdf>. Accessed on: May 5, 2013.

SILVA, Mariana Saraiva Chaves. **Adoption by Homosexual Couples**. Monograph presented at the conclusion of the Graduation Course at the Pontifical Catholic University of Rio Grande do Sul/Porto Alegre. 2007. Available at:<http://www3.pucrs.br/pucrs/files/uni/poa/direito/graduacao/tcc/tcc2/trabalhos2007_1/marianasaraiva.pdf>. Accessed on: May 5, 2013.

SILVA, Mariana Saraiva Chaves. **Adoption by Homosexual Couples**. Monograph presented at the conclusion of the Graduation Course at the Pontifical Catholic University of Rio Grande do Sul/Porto Alegre. 2007. Available at: <http://docplayer.com.br/6655431-A-adocao-por-pares-homosexuals.html>. Accessed on: November 14, 2013.

SIQUEIRA, Alessandro Marques de. **The concept of family throughout history and the maintenance obligation.** 2010. Available at:< http://jus.com.br/artigos/17628/o-conceito-de-familia-ao-longo-da-historia-e-a-obrigacao-alimentar>. Accessed on November 12, 2012.

SIQUEIRA, Alessandro Marques de. **The Concept of Family Throughout History and the Obligation to Feed** . 2010. Available at:<https://jus.com.br/artigos/17628/o-conceito-de-familia-ao-longo-da-historia-e-a-obrigacao-alimentar>. Accessed on: November 12, 2012.

SOUSA, Alipio de. **Down with Heterosexist Fundamentalism - Critique of a Fraud in the Scientific and Moral Fields**. Available at:<http://www.cchla.ufrn.br/alipiosousa/index arquivos/ARTIGOS%20ACADEMICOS/ARTIGOSPDF/ABAIXO%20O%20FUNDAMENTALISMO%20HETEROSSEXISTA.pdf>. Accessed on: November 14, 2013.

TEPEDINO. Gustavo. **Topics in civil law**. 3ª . updated edition. Rio de Janeiro: Renovar, 2004. p.372.

VASCONCELLOS, Ana Carolina Esteves**. The Evolution of the Concept of Family in Post-Modernity**. Monograph presented at the conclusion of the Graduation Course at Fundapao De Ensino "Euripides Soares Da Rocha" Centro Universitario Euripides De Marilia - Univem Faculty of Law. 2014.Disponivelem:<http://aberto.univem.edu.br/bitstream/handle/11077/1169/A%20EVOLU%C3%87%C3%83O%20DO%20CONCEITO%20DE%20FAM%C3%8DLIA%20NA%20P%C3%93S%20MODERNIDADE.pdf?sequence=1>. Accessed on: December 15, 2015.

VASSAL, Mylene Gloria Pinto. **The Evolution of Families and its Reflections on Society and the Law.** Serie Aperfeipoamento de Magistrados 12t Familia do Seculo XXI - Aspectos Juridicos e Psicanaliticos. Available at:<http://www.emerj.tiri.jus.br/serieaperfeicoamentodemagistrados/paginas/series/ 12/familiadoseculoXXI 126.pdf.>. Accessed on: December 15, 2012.

VENOSA, Silvio de Salvo. **Homoaffectivity and the Law**. In Magister Magazine of Civil Law and Civil Procedure, No. 39, Nov/Dec 2010. Porto Alegre: Ed. Magister, 2010.

WALD, Arnoldo. **The New Family Law**. 15ª ed. Sao Paulo: Saraiva. 2004. p. 09/10.

WELTER, Pedro Belmiro. **Equality between biological and socio-affective filiation**.
Sao Paulo: Editora Revista dos Tribunais, 2003.

Printed by Books on Demand GmbH, Norderstedt / Germany